Praise for *wine for a shotgun*

I defy you to read the first three poems in *wine* ╵
Marty McConnell close, forever. —Norman Lear, le

It's said that "In wine, there is truth." In *wine for a shotgun*, Marty McConnell offers a rich, full-bodied, complex bouquet of truths from the delirious edge of the everyday disaster, the hangover of the nuclear family, and the giddy elation of desire and transgression. The "wine" of the title should tip you off: This book is intoxicating.
—Daphne Gottlieb, author of *15 Ways to Stay Alive*

Marty McConnell is utterly fearless. She'll tell you gentle truths with great lyric imagination and she'll tell the harder truths with fire-hardened honesty rare in contemporary poetry. When I read these lines, "...I was struck still/ and wordless by the light...", I was struck still, but not wordless: This is a brave and beautiful book and Marty McConnell has placed herself very firmly among the best poets of her (very talented) generation.
—Thomas Lux, director of the McEver Writers Program at Georgia Institute of Technology

There is wild and wicked joy in the pages of *wine for a shotgun*, and an uncanny ability to find forms that capture experiences most of us would not be able to acknowledge, much less celebrate. Marty McConnell's radiant candor shines through, using her trademark rueful humor; I can't remember a collection where color rises up so fiercely in tarot, myth, and lonely-lovely song. These sexy and heart-thumping poems can persuade even the most jaded of readers to want to be "a sucker ... for hot wax and a good old-fashioned spanking," and that is a very noble wish, to "make shame an outlaw, a stranger, [to] make us the fool." —Aimee Nezhukumatathil, author of *Lucky Fish*

Marty McConnell's *wine for a shotgun* is a collection of rock and roll epistles written from the interior mind to the harlequin citizens of the multiverse. All our static notions of man-woman, eros and mathematics are undone and remade into these boisterous, gutsy, and loving poems. I get the sense McConnell might put her poetic fist through glass and steel if there were a heart worth touching on the other side. It's about time this book came out. It's one I've been waiting for. —Patrick Rosal, author of *Boneshepherds*

Marty McConnell is a revelatory spirit, seemingly unaware of her absolute mastery of light and lyric and her enviable ability to sway her readers with a dizzying meld of grace, ferocity and staggering insight. This is revolutionary work—exquisitely crafted, with an addictive narrative flow that snares and enthralls. Once you've entered these pages, you will know where poetry is headed. And you will be changed.
—Patricia Smith, author of *Blood Dazzler*

Marty McConnell's *wine for a shotgun* offers both argument and apologia addressed to the self and to a world presumed to be tragically deaf. That's one reason "because" loops through this collection like a noose strung around the poet's neck—around yours and mine, too—its end knot held tight in the speaker's sweaty hands. The "ordinary" but secret "monster" staring back in this book's mirror gives wine and shotgun blast to the "exploding bird" of the human heart. McConnell maps our aching hunt for an elusive "fidelity" whose smile shape shifts to grimace just before its toothy kiss.
—Kevin Stein, Illinois Poet Laureate

Cover art by Debra Hampton, *Still Life with Rifle*, 2011
Book design by Sarah Stec

ISBN: 978-0-9850946-2-1

Printed in the United States of America for EM Press, LLC.
First printing, 2012

EM Press
24041 S. Navajo Dr.
Channahon, IL 60410
www.em-press.com

wine
for a
shotgun

table of contents

the fidelity of disagreement

because there are seven kinds of loneliness
the receptionist keeps a basket of candy
by her desk. I keep my hair long
out of some poorly sublimated need

for tangible accomplishment. on Tuesdays
the local crackhead calls me Miss America.
most afternoons, the jobless gather in pockets

to shout compliments to each other across Sheridan.
it sounds a great deal like seagulls calling
other seagulls over the lake, or more

accurately, around the ascending buildings
where they screech directions, one
to the other, headed for water that is not
the river, past the bridge and the Picasso,

over the heads of the unlisteners, headphones
tucked into our ears, and this is the first
loneliness. in the dream, I pull away slowly,

and you stand there, very still. when I turn
the corner, you are still there, and the next,
still there in the rearview, then it's not a car at all

but a movie, you're in an airport in San
Francisco, on an ex-lover's couch in Seattle,
it's unseasonably cold for October, even
for Chicago. there's too much room

on the mattress and your shoes sit panting
in the closet. what do I know about loneliness?
you're on your way home to me

and a kitchen where the overhead light
sighs to a dim, the spoons tuck
their worn faces away. it's best

to argue in person, so you can see
where to aim the knives. this
is the third. I don't know what
I would name a child. four. across

the train, a grown man memorizes the pattern
of a girl's school uniform skirt. a shirt button
is about to come undone. he leans forward

in his seat, our train a compression chamber
draining. five. somebody says, *you have
to show up early if you want to get*

the chocolate. I want to name this
something other than sorrow, tell you
I have a bird behind each knee. one
is always in a panic. the other, most often

asleep. I wish I could tell you that I know
what I'm doing. was I ever a woman
who could shave her head

without flinching? I was. six. we have time
for mistakes. the men on the street orbit
the employment office in a set rotation

visible to none of them. what
loneliness is left? you have
the most beautiful face.

the Lovers

wish it were simple. where
are their hands? how
over such intense distance

do they touch? paired
in their ability to harm.
noise from the parade

is overwhelming. by all
accounts, they are happy.
she wears his mustache

with aplomb, he dances
as if still in his mother's
satin pumps. in their one body,

they carry a drumline
of options, pounding
like thunder. *arriba!* the crowd

is enthralled. their hair
plaits itself into oceans.
a surfer emerges

for his turn, simple magic. wave,
belly, feet, turn. the lovers
are exhausted. horns blow

from all directions. they are not lovers
at all but birds, governed by wind
as much as by instinct. on a rooftop

in Bushwick, a man calls his flock
back to their cages. *what was it,*
the lover says, *you wanted me to know?*

nothing, the lover says. *nothing.*

Five of Swords, for all my death girls

Betsy's in the second stall practicing
with a plastic razor, so I lie on the floor
to listen for the janitor, the cart's

loose wheel squeaking our names down
the evening-empty hallway. the weeks
she was at Lutheran General, I didn't

go to visit. but I know from her stories
what the doors looked like, closing,
how they strapped her to the bed
for her own protection. we're 17

and I adore her despair. I think she's shining,
fearless, carving herself a body that's nothing
but light. on the way home, she lets me
drive. tells me there's a trick

to disintegrating in increments subtle enough
not to trip the alarm wires, to hiding cigarettes
and death from therapists and parents and this,

all my girls have had down: how to go and go
until the night is too fragile or grimy
and then the fanfare, the wild dive

from the spire, the water tower, the clock
yanking its hands back, how to dangle
from the spotlight once everybody's
watching. 1999: we lie on Angie's futon

searching the phonebook for institutions
that will take her without insurance, curl
our bodies into still commas of want
to wait for morning. they take

her shoelaces, and her cigarettes, and I watch.
they give her forms and more forms
and I watch. they walk her to the room

with its single bed and single dresser
and unsmashable mirror and I ride
the long, high buzz of the door back

to New York. 2003: Georgiana is an expert
in suicide and poetry. her medicine cabinet rattles
like a jar of vengeful bees. she wants me
to find her. all our idols are martyrs, not one of them

a saint. her hair drops like cabernet all the way
to her waist. and how she needs me. my simple body
becomes bread in her mouth, I'm whiskey,
an obliteration who'll get up in the morning

to call the hospital and make coffee. oh,
my pretty ones in love with the beast
of disappearing, there are many ways

to give birth. not one is without pain.
there are almost as many ways to die
as there are to love. tonight, I drink to you

who chose to keep going, who moved
through my body like a chemical
I could not keep. the night stands outside
like a hungry dog on an old chain, the scent

of lilies rising from the half moons of his teeth.
go ahead. tuck your babies into bed
and lovers' hair behind their soft ears, as if
there's nothing left to fear.

fable telling how night invented
herself out of sound

nights I was afraid of the moon
or spiders or the janitor

who was always whistling,
I would cross the long hall

like a river, like Jordan
in the song, toward the bed

where my parents slept. I'd stand
by my mother's head for seconds

though it seemed my whole life,
perched in the dim of their

paired breathing, the light
from the double windows,

moonlight filtered through the oak,
laced across them and the porch roof

we were to climb out on and down
in case of fire, and she would wake

and say *Martha, what is it?* and I
would whisper *I'm scared* though

I wasn't anymore, in that room
with the platform bed and the breathing

and I would climb in between them,
their cotton pajamas hushing

across the sheets. the air
from their mouths was the air

in dreams, cloud-like and solid
as spun candy. the dark

of their room was the dark
of the moon when it is there

but hidden, the shadow
of our planet draped across it

like a shroud or the caul
a mother lifts to watch

her first daughter's pink mouth
release its originating scream.

when your very pregnant sister
sits down at her own table

resist the urge to hand her a photograph of your father
in the 1980s, on Halloween, with his co-workers, dressed
as a heavy metal rockstar. do not point out his hand

on the accountant's small waist, or ask
if she remembers the woman from his running club.
you were the only daughter gullible enough

to believe it an honor to fold newsletters
at Saturday morning meetings while your sisters

watched cartoons and your mother vacuumed.
even if your brother-in-law leaves the room

to watch baseball on the TV. even if the cactus
holds out its spiny hands as if say, *when, when,*
when. remember it is only your story to tell

because you know no one else will, and in this way
you are your mother in unflattering
pants, saint medals dangling

from the rearview, meeting after meeting, library
board, PTA, church council, and your father

in Springfield, Peoria, across town
working late—how you find yourself

them, the martyr, the philanderer, how strange
to be this stitched-together beast drinking tea
with your sister and niece-to-be. no matter what

shade of purple the kitchen tiles turn, or how
the air turns the consistency of jello, don't use
the cactus' thin spine to split your puckering

seam—she didn't ask. don't lay all your sorrows
like kittens on the table, a litter of raccoons

scratching the polished top, their faces
so furiously bright, so perfectly masked.

Two of Swords

I want to write your body
into music. to rhyme
until your thighs become tawdry
psalms, become songs

the night holds between its whistling lips
breathing out. I want an arch
from your back and an alto moan pulling
across the scarlet children

inked into your chest, a stand-up bass' low note,
stretched – if I were a genius. or
an alchemist, or a man who could blow glass
into asphodels, into aliens

and chandeliers, the soft trigger
of your body might trust me. each
distanced molecule gather itself
into one daredevil note that sends the cats

in the alley racing for home. my god, I love you.
I'm a melted orchestra puddled at the base
of your throat. each reticent inch of you
is an altar I want to put

my mouth to. do not pull away. if there
are monsters here, I will string them
into the harp of my ribs. I will use
these hands to draw

and tune them. I will play them,
woman, into wind.

the fidelity of Cincinnati

in the days when any boy with a ponytail and strong jawline was compared
to Brad Pitt, I met a boy with a ponytail and a jaw of moderate

proportions and made him my hairstylist. I made him my hairstylist
and he told me about his girlfriend Anya for whom he drew

astonishingly hot baths. Anya was Russian. I pictured her in the bath
swilling vodka, angry as he said she often was. he was

my hairstylist. he broke up with Anya. I didn't ask about the vodka
when we started fucking. Anya was Russian, I pictured her

large, with a flock of red hair. I wanted him to draw me a bath, hot,
but I never asked. I wasn't Russian. he'd cut my hair

late on a Friday and we'd fuck in the back of the salon and then
go dancing. he'd work the dance floor as women flocked

to admire my still-fabulous post-coital hair.
he'd cut my hair, dye it some months redder

some months blonder. by the time I left to move back
to Chicago I was next door to platinum. the women

in the club would compliment my hair
and he'd give them half-off

coupons for their first visit. we'd go back
to his enormous apartment in the worst neighborhood

in the city and fuck. I never met Anya.
I pictured her walking around this apartment he told me

they'd shared. sat in the dry bathtub spinny
from the shots we'd done

at the club. he never ran me a bath. I never asked. the women
loved his ponytail. his strongish jaw. my hair. Anya

showed up once at a party he threw, but I
was upstairs. his friends kept us

in separate parts of the house until she left.
I didn't know she was there, red

lipstick on the glass they said she threw
against the wall as she left. he could only come

if you called his name. I was straight
then. everyone at the party was high, I realize

now. he made furniture and sold it
to childless gay men. some people thought

he was gay. Anya crashed the party, drank half
the champagne, smashed a glass

and left. she was Russian. he knew my friend
from high school. it's how we met. she said

he wouldn't kick anything pretty
out of bed. I took him

to a wedding. we were bored
so we fucked in the stairwell. I did it mostly

to have a story to tell. he came to visit
a year after I moved

back to Chicago. before I left, he started fucking
my friend Cora. this was before

we broke up. I never really enjoyed vodka.
the bathtub was enormous. when I kissed a woman

for the first time it reminded me
of Cora. he got addicted

to coke, he came to visit me in Chicago, told me
his therapist said going cold-turkey off coke

often leads to suicide. he came to visit after I started
kissing women and got angry

that I didn't pay him enough attention. I saw Cora
years later in Chicago

and gave her the poem I'd written
about her boots and strong chin. years later

I heard he moved to the South, got married and gave up
hair. he married some Southern girl, didn't

marry Anya. I never got to meet her. she was Russian
and he drew her baths so hot

they steamed the long hallway, the furniture was designed
for the childless, I had bruises on my legs

the shape of its so fashionable edges, I had no
children, I am not

Russian, I dyed my hair back, he didn't
kill himself, it was another

ten years before I tried my first line of coke.
I heard he got married, heard he got clean, moved

south, sells those ads that run before movies. I hear
there's good money in that.

trespasses

I sit in my beautiful sister's beautiful kitchen
and finger the stones in my pockets. rocks
our mother gave me, said *hold these, they're*

so heavy. my sister has colors, green
the kitchen, turquoise the living room,

dining room, a blue bedroom,
silver nursery. nursery. without
the stones, would I too

be ordinary? the piano in our parents' basement
goes untuned for years. I write my other sister
a letter that starts, *do you feel destroyed*

by the way we were raised? but it never
gets sent. her wedding dress was the color
of clementines. she too has a cradle, and more

than one apron. I pretend the stones
are lemons, roll them in my hands
when everyone else is in bed.

.

ordinary is a compliment. a husband
who brings you tea and rubs your head.
means you don't lose things

when you move, means you don't move
because of something you lost, but because

you're making a human or the new place
has a better yard or view or schools. you
have troubles too, but the clementines

never go bad on your counter. if you had
a piano, it would play in tune.

.

some nights I devour each stone
until my belly rolls with noise, until
I am full and pendulous with everything

I am trying not to say. I am trying not to say
fair or *unfair*, not to say *blinders* or *caution,*

falling rocks ahead. trying not to pick
my teeth like playing a piano with broken keys,
and I am succeeding. I am succeeding.

•

I tie an apron around my neck. I peel lemons
with my feet. I roll the piano over and over
until the strings ping from their sockets

like floss yanking out baby teeth. I cradle
the biggest stone I can find like an infant
then swallow it whole. now I can sleep.

•

I brought you a clementine. its seeds
are like tiny stones. when our mother gave me
the rocks, she said, *take these.*
but I heard *keep.*

the fidelity of yes

things keep disappearing.
there are so many lighters
and then none

once I find a candle.
some days I think
the days are coming on

too fast. some days I think,
why would anyone
want to sit in the same room

as me. some days I think,
the water is perfect. let's go
for a swim. dip our faces

in the lake made of forsythia.
or of gin. why does it always
come back to booze. your first love

is coming for a visit this weekend.
I will let her sleep on our floor
if she asks to. I am a city

of yeses. I can deny you
nothing. also, I cannot fix you
or mend your solitude,

even the part that is mostly
my fault. I'm broken
and I won't find a therapist

because if that doesn't work
we're down to chicken wire
and hymnals and you're a Jew

and I'm no good on the farm
or anywhere that requires faith
in the rain. the corn

was so late this year, the farm stand
started selling rocks. this is what I do
for a living: figure out what people

will pay for, and make it pretty.
this doesn't work with you.
you're as manageable as the weather

and as pure. it's upsetting. I'm used
to a good deal of climate control. if we
were a song, I could write in

a chorus for respite. whole measures
of easy repetition, sha la la.
some days I want to take us back

to syllables. to unpack my guts
like an accordion. you're perfect
and I'm a genius or you're perfect

at making me believe cyanide
is wine, or vice versa. either way,
my bones wake me up every hour

you're gone. I don't get a lot of sleep
these days. I write things on my body
so they won't escape. let's go to Paris

where they'd eat us for breakfast.
let's go back to the farm
and get us some rocks

to chew. let's go to the church
where all the pews are set backward.
we'll put razors in the prayer books

and call ourselves even
with whoever made us.

the Magician is a drag king

there's a mouthful of man
where my cunt used to be. note
how I lean against this pole

like I've got the right chromosomes
for this game. like I was born
with this name. I guess
you could call it a compulsion

but tell me you don't codeswitch
from morning bed to subway wait
to secretary to barstool to bed again—
the stretch from femme to boi to butch to man's

the feathered edge of a scalpel, so close
the sweat even smells the same. and here
I am, your rock god andromorph.
you want more than the cock

in my pants and that's good, that's
what everybody's looking for, a little
freak in your Friday, a shapeshifter lover

so you've got every excuse to call
the wrong name, to name the wrong
body, the wrong end, to want
what boils low in the belly

where the good words don't go
but the letters tat themselves together
like lace under old ladies' fingers into *um*
and *oh* and the thousand practiced

hesitations—I like to let a little nipple
show, sometimes, to flash the twat
behind the dildo. transgression's the infant
I give birth to every time the stagelights

go up. you're a sucker
for the sideshow and I'm your spirit
gum queen, your strapped-down
goddess, your husband with a little extra

in between, I'm Venus with a goatee
I markered on myself, you can't mock
this, I made this, my playlist
is gay bliss, go on DJ,

break it down—everybody
wants somebody. every body wants
some body. everybody wants. some.
body. a girl's got to use every tool

she's got and beg, barter, or steal
the rest. come on, you know you want
to be transformed. you know
you want to be a star. stick whatever

you want in those slacks. pack, bind,
beard if you want—what matters
is the saunter. the walk. how you carry
what you've got. the snake

around your waist is incapable
of lying, uroboros at the strip
joint, satan at the cabaret. unravel
what makes a man a man. name one

thing I can't buy at the five and dime
or the costume shop. when I take
the streets as me or the dude I now know

I can be, the sidewalks clear. this swagger
is a 21st century alchemy. say you know me.
tell me now: who's the man.

when your grandmother mistakes your girlfriend for a man

do not rise up over the dinner table
like a sequin tornado

or a burning flag. it is Christmas.
though the forks

curl their tines into tiny silver fists
and the frost-

rimmed windows blink in embarrassment,
focus on your lover

as she clears her throat, extra low, passes the salt
to your grandmother

who thanks the young man with the strange
haircut and delicate

hands. this is no time for declarations and no one's
seemed to notice

though the milk's gone solid in the pitcher
and your father

is suddenly fascinated by the unmoving air
in the other room.

your mouths do not move, except
to chew. this is family,

this is holiday, there are no affairs, no
addictions, your family

crest reads in elaborate embroidery
the less said,

the better. though your father did offer once
to pay for your therapy

back when no one you knew was in therapy
and there was no way

you were going to talk to a stranger about things
you'd never say

to your mother, even drunk, even on Easter. so
to say something now

about what might be a mistake, or just the easiest way
to explain a mohawk

would be bringing sand to the bank. unprofitable
and a little bit

insane. you study your lover's chin. the tweezers wince
under the sink.

she could be a boy, you think. apocalyptic Christian
emails aside,

maybe your grandmother is progressive. astute
in her own

Southern, incidental way. your voice offering her
the butter is a punk band

playing an abortion clinic. all feedback
and nobody wants you.

she's your grandmother. she's nearly 100.
your uncle

took thirty years to get sober. your grandfather died
still owning the manual

to every piece of machinery he'd ever owned.
you still

don't know how to make any kind of pie.
there are no

family recipes. in the far corner of your liver
your other grandmother

looks up from her patient sectioning
of a grapefruit,

offers you a chunk of your own atrophied
tongue, trembling

at the edge of her serrated spoon.

daily bread

the mother is purple.
the carpet is spruce. it is Tuesday
and already things require
a screwdriver. the ironing board
come loose. purple is Lent, Advent, waiting

for the Big Happening. with the screwdriver,
she pries open the stuck drawer in the chest.
to moonwalk is to move backward on the balls
of one's feet. Tuesday and spruce means
the carpet needs to be cleaned. the ironing board
squeaks, its metal legs resisting. tightening

requires the screwdriver. good tool.
good Tuesday. a porcupine
defends itself by letting its quills
attach to the attacker. spruce
is a conifer covered in needles.
each tool in the basement

has its place. the mother
has never moonwalked, but knows
where the screwdriver goes. nothing
in her house has a lock that can't be broken.

•

the juice of blueberries
is adamantly purple. nothing
gets it out of the carpet. red wine,
stained teeth, Tuesday.

a man comes to the house and is
refused. a man comes to the house
to repair the water heater. a man

comes home to find dinner
on the stove, the children
in their sleeping clothes.
the screwdriver sleeps on a hook

in the basement. does not moonwalk
or sing. the chest folds its fat lip,
does not sing. the children

eat their peas, do not sing. the man
does not sing, nor the mother,
nor the porcupine in the yard
smoothing her quills.

.

spruce as in evergreen. as in Christmas
wreath, as in enormous plots of land
visited by men who get to wield axes
once a year, take down a tree
to plant like a flag in the foyer. top

with a star, an angel, wire to the wall
so that cat won't knock it over. the whole house
smells like wood. needles shoulder
into the carpet, into the children's feet.
the porcupine rejoices in the yard.
some might call it a moonwalk.

.

what's been pried open can be
repaired. purple is the blush
of a new bruise. spruce
the whistle of it fading. who

am I to lift the screwdriver
from its hook. to walk its wedge
down the length of my thigh.
why are the locks the only things

singing here. why am I the only one here
who can pronounce the word *trespass*.
why would anybody think
they'd be saved by the truth.

disclosure

hello body, you old crime scene, den
of exhausted arsonists. there's a wick
in the next room shaped
like a girl and she wants us
to kiss her like they do
in fairy tales where the long sleep

is a stand-in for sexual
awakening. this is our
shared adolescence, our awkward
years, true we have no horse
but don't imagine the prince
did not also hesitate at the thicket

of briars, the hermetic glass box,
thinking *what if she doesn't wake*
and I just kissed a dead girl, what
if her lips are glossed shut
with dust—fairy tales almost never
involve fire. body, body, what

have we got to lose? the girl rarely
comes to bed before dawn now
and always smelling then of ash. here
is a match, go run a bath of gasoline
and lead her to it by the hand. if a river
can burn then why not a story, why not

a room where bodies collide only
at a distance. nobody said
it was going to be easy except
for the stories but then one of us has got
to be the hero, and what does that make
the other when nobody's a maiden

here, and nobody's got a horse, all you've got
are these hands and a bathtub full of fuel—
come on, body. make the tiles testify
to heat, put mouth to the mayhem,
let it never be said we refused
to go down in flames.

Queen of Rods on top

the harness holds my hips like hands,
a trapeze artist's first practice. if you hold
very still, you can hear the world opening
like a well oiled door. the body
is laid out like a map of the city, some
places gridded, some whorled like the side
of a fist, like a cul de sac where the houses
all face inward, each unshuttering
its windows in turn, knowing
something big is on its way.

the Hierophant explains

how could a right-minded man
not worship what connects the body
to the earth? heaven and death
in one flesh package—the rising
arch, the tombstone toes—to swallow
it whole, to be trampled
as by a god's elephantine step, adorned,
adored, the chorus of diminutive
bones, oar of the corpus, motor
and source, podiatric dream,
let me take you
in the mouth, stop this reedy noise
in favor of skin and nail, those
garish prayer flags. cast off
the nylon and leather. let me at you
raw and aloft, for once
without the burden of a breathing
corpse's heft. you miniature
gods of foxtrot and stomp, every callus
is a roadmap my grateful tongue
follows. the blood hums
through the heel and anterior
tibial artery, a tune I have
from childhood, a metatarsal
lullaby, a love song that knows dirt
and weight and the full length
of a leg, the long fall of a body
toward its holiest
and most irresistible part.

thine

I never meant to be a monster,
then quickly was. in fleeing,
we only become more ourselves

and it's rarely good. maybe I wanted
to understand the fruit of it, the flesh
and seed, what could have been better

than us, our snowmen and piano
recitals and pocket bread.
because the other had no face

or name in the story, I had
to become her. find my father
in a skin no one would recognize

as his, make her in this new body
no one would suspect. bald
and unadorned, I was barely

a woman, let alone a mistress,
but I was and was, I was fruit
gyrating on the vine, I knew

exactly what I was doing.

·

I don't think anyone sets out to become
a philanderer. a monster. a whore. no matter

how badly raised, few
little boys will say *an adulterer*
when asked what they want to be

when they grow up. few little girls
gyrate on the piano, say, *slut*.

·

but here we are, fucking in the bathtub.
the wrong man but the right
monster, it feels good to be damaged

in manageable ways.
the piano is so out of tune it can barely
be played, but the bench

holds a body's weight like a champion.
the truth? an affair is junkie
love. sweet bread that will take your teeth

and leave you aching for fruit. and fruit
will leave you hungry for milk,
and milk for wine, and wine

for a shotgun or a bowl of arsenic
soup. here's a secret: every monster
is lonelier than you. every piano starts out

playing in tune. come
a little closer. I'd like to know you.

the fidelity of the painfully adolescent
(song for seventh grade)

and it is true, Susie Hoffman, that your dress
has as many ruffles as a debutante's
wedding cake. that when we sang "Like

an Eagle" at the grade school graduation,
I wanted with all my wanting to be
an alto so I could stand on the same riser

as you. but I, polyester A-line soprano,
had to sway on the top riser with Phoebe
who snorted when she breathed and never

went to slumber parties even
when she was invited, some kind
of religious thing or because her mother

once caught her eating paste. we're 12 now,
and I think we should not be blamed
for what tasted good to us

in second grade. oh, Susie. you
are in the smart kids class with me
and still the boys slide notes into

your locker. nobody makes fun of your backpack
or throws your lunch money into the grass
behind the soccer field. you're the only person

who ever gave me a nickname. and yes
it was a mean one that gave the boys
new ammunition for the playground but I

didn't care because it was what you called me,
and Susie, when you called me, I came.

the Emperor likes it rough

the scepter's a baton
in the right hands. in particular,
the Emperor likes to be bitten. likes
tall ones with good
teeth. but the Emperor's
a switch, from day to day
you never know which end
will be up, there's a pattern
but it's not for you to know.
yours is to show up
for the breathplay, for the
discipline. the Emperor's a man
who knows what he needs, where
the bruises won't be seen, how
to bind and when to accede.
grab the skin just above
the left kidney and squeeze.
the Emperor's a sucker
for asphyxiation, for hot wax
and a good old-fashioned
spanking. yes, he likes to be
held down. yes, the roses are there
for their thorns. the safeword
is mayday. he wants to be sore
the next day, wants
to remember you
in the shoulders and neck,
across each haunch. the Emperor
is not a pony. the Emperor
is not your daddy. the Emperor
will give you the world and you
will give it right back.

when it comes out in therapy
that he never wanted children

remember the doll with the music box
inside, the cranberry velvet dress, half

your size, all that hair, the lashes,
eyes so real, so begging to be touched

that you did, did touch, the left rolling back
into her porcelain head, the new

favorite, the gift you hadn't set down
since picking her up from next

to the stocking blooming with licorice
and an orange, the O your mouth formed

when the eye fell back, the tin song
still unreeling from her torso, how

your mother found you on the couch,
crying, tilting her gently upside down,

to the left and to the right, listening
to the eye fall not quite back

into its socket, having *ruined it,*
ruined everything—how your father,

late that night, far into
the quiet, glued the glass eye back

into place in the basement
where he'd taught you

and your sisters to hammer
a nail straight into wood, where

you'd hammer for hours, nail
after nail, flat head, diamond point,

pennyweight, making nothing
but a racket that drove your mother

to the piano, glued the eye back
with only the thinnest rim

of glue showing, sat her back
on the chair in your room, a porcelain

hand open on each knee, offering
after offering.

when your ex-girlfriend's sister corners you in the kitchen

do not scream *fire* or slam the oven door
on your hand. the empty wine bottles
by the trash can only seem to be rattling.
the teapot is not actually screeching

like a rape whistle. yes, you are caught
between the window and the fridge,
drinkless. yes, she wants to know

what your *queer status* is. and yes,
the kitchen door did just shiver
on its hinges. no, that didn't
happen. are those carolers

at the door? or just the broken stereo.
in the next room, your somewhat husband
tosses back another vodka and laughs.
you can hear the bottle clink against

the glass, can hear a garage door open down
the block, hear the neighbor's children
turning in their beds. a woman in front of you

is breathing impatiently. she is angry.
the crumbs on the counter scramble
into an arrow pointing to the door,
the door under which your ex-

girlfriend's husband's Irish tongue slides
and kittens across the floor toward
the woman's solid, khaki-covered ankles

and you say *what?* and she says many
things about privilege and moving
through the world like a straight
girl and confusing adolescents with your

loose definitions and when you say
weren't you married? like, to a dude? she says
*yes. but I never went back. you have
to choose.* and you can hear

the filaments in the ceiling fixture
sizzle, the glue under the linoleum starting
to bubble. all the liquor in the house is in

the other room and your mouth is a desert
with a side of sand, you are stranded
on the moon with a woman who thinks
you can make the atmosphere breathable

just by believing it, or rather you
are on the moon and she's back
in the spaceship saying *take*

*off your helmet. the weather's beautiful
from where I'm standing. really,
you should go ahead and try it.*

the Chariot in love

there is a red box in my bedroom
for the disposal of needles.
there is a woman in my bed

with a body made of flowers.
they feel like thorns to her,
like weeds. part of me thinks

she is dying. another part says *no,*
that's how we sleep now. the hormones
are new, but the story is old: Tiresius

was a man, then a woman, then
a man. punishment, prophecy,
redemption. I've begun guessing

at the gender of lamp-posts. of couches.
of calendars. watching the jaws of men
on the train, studying their shoulders,

the shrug in their lean. I've become
something different now, too. I watch
your body square into itself and think,

armor. the temperature of your skin in sleep
says *fever, flight, release.* we leave
the windows open all winter. I am cold

but you are here. I never learn
to push the needle into the meat
of your thigh. does this make me

a coward, or the man in the moon?
you're extraordinary. last spring,
my sister ripped out half a garden

of blossomless poppies
because a neighbor told her
anything with thorned stems

and thorned leaves is a weed.
no matter what answer
you give the gods, something

will be granted and something taken
away. I would like someone to teach me
a new way to pray. I fold photographs

of you as a girl into postcards
and mail them to orphans. you are
your own daughter. everyone

earns their body somehow. what
do we do now?

•

*transform, metamorphose, transmute, transmogrify, convert,
transfigure*: to change a thing into a different thing. *transform*
implies a major change in form, nature, or function
{*transformed* a small company into a corporate giant.}
metamorphose suggests an abrupt or startling change induced
by or as if by magic or a supernatural power {awkward girls
metamorphosed into swannish ballerinas.} *transmute* implies
transforming into a higher element or thing {attempted
to *transmute* lead into gold, body into deity.} *transmogrify*
suggests a strange or preposterous metamorphosis {a story
in which a frog is *transmogrified* into a photograph once
thought lost, now reappearing as an ad for feminine hygiene
products.} *convert* implies a change fitting something for
a new or different use or function {*converted* the study into a
nursery, the bed into a boarding house.} *transfigure* implies
a change that exalts or glorifies {joy, or maybe it was the
hormones, *transfigured* her face.}

•

love, may the body you are becoming hold fewer
cruel boundaries. may its territories admit my hands,
hormones taking down fences like boys in cars

with baseball bats swinging at mailboxes.
dear mystery, dear mythological
shapeshifter, may I adore you

in any skin, inherited or built.
there is a hair below your chin
that I love to study. it is like
a small flag invented by an army

wildly outnumbered but with the very
best uniforms. their boots punched with holes
but polished to a sheen in which they can see

their gorgeous reflections. a god's
perfect monsters, they stomp
through your bloodstream, set up camp

at the base of your spine where I tuck
my knee while sleeping. they are not sure
how to love me. a body untransformed,
transfigured only by time and afternoons

at the gym. may you be able
to remind them, I was here first.
or at least, I love you more.

•

you are not a war. there is nothing
to be won here. you asked me once
what my ruin is. what could make me
a monster. I didn't answer. the answer is,

fear. I am that ordinary. I was born
like this. but I have invented new ways
to pray. the clock is a liar who dissolves
in the light. the shower is resurrection central.

your mouth is a storehouse of surrogate
bones, you grow fruit trees and crocus
in the back of your throat. give me
your moonshoulders, the stars all over

your body, and the keys. hand over
the map. you choose the road. I can keep
both wheels on the ground, I can hold us.
the book says, *remember. victory is just*

the beginning. we'll make a banner
from your binding shirt, collect my shed hair
for the seams. my love, my sphinx, my vanishing
point, I am not perfect. but I was built for this.

individuation, Wisconsin

convinced that I should have been born
a redhead, I decide one summer to become
a tomboy. refuse all shoes, climb
the weeping willow whose long arm
arcs out over the lake. but my soft
feet tear and the bark stripes my thighs
with welts like a disease so I come down
a girl, defeated, slide rocks the size
of my grandmother's breasts
inside my thin shirt. move slowly
up the hill toward the kitchen full
of my mother, standing there
waiting, with her own face on.

the fidelity of distance

I hate that you leave but adore
being missed. the horses
in the field between us face

one another, each daring
the other to run. do horses dare?
nothing stops them. not the trees,
not the senseless dark, the fence

is long and what horse reasons distance
anyway. you are not a horse. I have never
taken off into the dark on anything's

back. we're not our fathers. I know
what it is to be faithful. you will
return. yesterday I wrote the word
home in the pit of my left foot. all day

the walking was like dancing
and the dancing, like your plane,
love, just as it left the ground.

the Tower

of all the deaths, falling. of all the senses,
touch. of all the touches, a hand
in the hair. of all the memories, a mother

braiding, hand over hand over hand.
these do not disappear. there's a boy

at the bottom of a well
drawing a picture of my spine.
or less obviously, my hunger.

it has been a long time
since we visited. for a while,
this was a matter of survival. now

I'm just being stubborn. leaning
over the edge, I catch sight

of his blonde head bent
as if in prayer or sleep
but I know better.

he is drawing everything
I gave away this year. this
is why I stay away. this

is why milk curdles at my lips,
why I wake in a river of sweat

in the frigid middle of January.
I've always been less afraid of heights
than of falling. less afraid of falling

than of opting to fall, of letting go
of the train platform, the quarry lip,
the mouth of the well, just to be done with it

already. his hair catches a slant of light
so well I remember the first boy I imagined

I'd have, and the boy his father was, and that fall
and the fall after. no one would believe me now

if I told them that dream. in it, I barely
recognize my own face. who was that girl?
how she jumped. what could she not have done.

on the tall ladder, painting the bedroom wall
a fine butter yellow, I am again

16, ripe with a pride stronger
than fear, hanging wreaths

in the sanctuary. they assigned boys
to the ladders but I insisted. up
nearly touching the cathedral ceiling

I kissed the god whose name I knew
and climbed down, safe. within a year

knew love, and betrayal. the boy
in the well remembers, plays a lullaby
on his tiny piano. raises his face

to me, and the light, and the woman
on fire behind me, braiding
and unbraiding my hair.

somebody

tell me a story that ends well
and is real. love

succeeding, cancer beaten, the recipe
that turns out perfect

the first time. men will compete
at anything, and I

will watch them on the TV. I want things
to turn out

right. so I watch *I Shouldn't Be Alive*
followed by

I Shouldn't Have Survived because
in the end

they did. and by "shouldn't" they don't mean
"I wish I hadn't,"

at least not in the interviews that make
the show. the boys

dragged out to the ocean's center in the dinghy
with no phone, no

snacks, no sunscreen, no mother—they all
made it back. and I

like that. I carry almonds just about everywhere
though they won't help

in the case of a bear attack. it's not that I don't
have hope, I do. it's just

that things have not been going my way of late.
I would like to stop

believing in love. or, alternatively, to have proof.
out of the hundreds

of people I know, I know two happy couples. I want
a deeply romantic attorney

and some licorice. I want a baby. I want to stand at the edge
of a rooftop overlooking the city

at dawn and say, I shouldn't have survived this.
but look,

just look at me now.

Temperance is a fan of polyamory

says big love's only a myth in public
opinion. says *yes* is the spell that most often
succeeds, is most often offered up in undistorted
tones, the om, the ah, jaws opening like a chest

into the void that calls back, that gifts
these bodies, a rapturous burden, these
bodies that lean and lean, knees that buckle

and mouths accepting no succor but mouth,
but devouring. pronounce it, the swearing
and sweating *yes*. Temperance says
you are a matched set, the beast

with four breasts, sweet monster with two
cocks, says neither love nor fucking
is binary, neither an either/or proposition,

says you are neither a god nor the devil
but a split minute synthesizing its own beauty
out of spit and hipbone, says this is the embrace
that conjures, this the exponential kiss, a holy

pornography (take that.) Temperance
says Temperance is different from moderation,
far from prohibition, says *an it harm none*, says

one foot in the ocean and one on the sand
means something about a bird, means
not scales but wings, says joy is no more a lie
than grief so bring someone luminous

and willing home from the bar, the bookstore,
the cab stand, or loose your great love's mouth
to another's *yes* and go home whole

and alone. call this its own bliss.
grow yourself a second heart
with chambers to spare, unwork envy
into its bitterest fragments, into what

you can swallow, can digest
to vitamin and mineral, give the clock
back its hands and the camera her eye,

lose track. Temperance loves an omnivore,
a smorgasbord, a little excess. Temperance says
if there's a heaven, it's a lot like orgasm,
so come. draw down the moon. tuck the sun

under your zealot's tongue and call it
a temple. the fourth house. Death.
Temperance says, come. what you thought

were walls are arms, and this room
is no myth, is your own heart, cradled
and about to bloom.

the Fool in her hunger

the lines we draw could be crayon,
could be coke, could be boxes
around lost causes—when
does the celebration of flesh

become fetish? the feast come carnage?
the hottest lesbian in Brooklyn is drunk
again. for her the lines are sun-drawn,
flesh-etched, the club explodes

with applause, she is drum
and bass refrain high in the chest, wet
and writhing, she wears her title
like a lantern well out into

the night, out onto the feral street
that does not care to know her name

.

deep. house. music. what moves you,
moves you, we stay

until the lyrics bleed through, until the body
is a crude object, mouth on the DJ, hips
indebted to the crush and the crew cuts

and the low-cut jeans and the tank tops that say
fuck you she's with me. we don't watch
where we put our hands we don't

wait for a moment to flower we are grinding
at the edge of the world. we've never been
this new. the beat drops, and we can move,

can call on God and Yemaya and Buddha
and the fool heart going boom, going hip
to thigh with the night until night

arches back with a cry, with an aye
from the spine and rocks like no one's
taken no one home before

.

we fling bodies against the night until it breaks
into math, into chorus, make a treehouse
of our feet and a constitution of tongues, make shame

an outlaw, a stranger, make us the fool—
I've researched the moon. I give the sun nothing
to go on about. take my chin

across her clavicle
like a cat, like a child who only
wants her way and knows

the rub, the rub, bone against skin
against skin against bone, the hair tugged hard
enough to sting, the divine

undivided breath of chest
against chest, we know home's a spot well
below the belly and it's sure not

the knees. we're all verb
here, all move and move again. dip
and roll back, tug close

and open, cut me another line
on the perfect glacier
of your lip. melt me a little piece,

a little piece
for this fresh glutton
I've become.

Seven of Pentacles
(reasons you shouldn't go home with me)

1

the apartment's on fire. I never bothered
to put it out.

2

I can't get the blue out of the sink
from when the last boy painted a tsunami
on my back.

3

I wanted the last boy to be
a girl. I'll do the same thing
to you.

4

when I say the apartment is on fire,
I mean your cheekbones are maps
that lead me backward in sleep
asking night for the rope on which hand
over hand I can climb out into a day
that doesn't break like an egg
when I hold it.

5

the tsunami was not
a metaphor. for a full day
I was the drowning wave.

6

you're a poet.

7

I'm trying to date outside the family.

8

in my world, a deadman
is somebody's grandfather. in yours,
it's when a dancer lands on the pavement
like a sack of laundry with bones.

9

you're an alcoholic.
I'm trying to date outside the family.

10

if the apartment were on fire, I imagine we'd move
to another city rather than salvage anything
from the soot and water damage.

you make me want to walk away.

11

you let a woman call another man's name
while you fucked her. that kind of twisted
generosity makes the handcuffs on the back
of my closet door shimmy like wind chimes.

12

see how you shouldn't tell me things.
imagine what would happen
if we were naked.

13

I considered seducing you once
when I crashed on your couch
but you were my then-lover's
best friend. you are my ex-
lover's best friend. did I mention
the apartment's on fire? the stones

on the altar have gathered themselves
into symbols of warning, the ash
and wax of wasted candles a rising creek
overflowing the sill, the faces
of every photograph curling in
on themselves, forehead to chin,

if I burn this city no refuge will have me
and your hands while sweet and temperate
are temporary shelter from the wave
that arrives without warning,
fully earned, endlessly deserved.

first betrayal

I do not remember hating my sister
but so the family anecdote goes and so
I go, we laugh, how much I hated
the baby, would bite her fat feet, could not

be left alone with the baby, the baby,
sooner or later we figure out
what we're worth, what gets our mothers
to not give us back. this is why

I am a tool belt. a box of raisins.
bail money and an inflatable mattress.
hi Mom. you'll never read this. remember

when I was eleven and Erin got so sick? I knew
it was my fault, or at least
I couldn't fix it, which was the same thing,
and when the mountains on the globe

I was making out of paper-mache
wouldn't stick, knew that I was
useless or somehow damaging, knew that if
I were any kind of sister, the kind

worth keeping, I would not have been
the Mussolini of our bedroom,
dictator of her small heart, standing over her

once while I was still bigger
and she hadn't gotten sick yet but was
unquestionably the favorite
or at least the most demanding, standing

with her arm twisted behind her
(I hope she doesn't remember) and making her say
she was *conceited*, I remember she

didn't know what the word meant and that
was just fine with me.

Eight of Swords
(what the pro dom doesn't say)

you come to me, your mouth
a treacherous shrine, home of cruel
fruit and heavy-breasted demons.
a man of faith who does not pray

is doomed to secular collapse, to fall into
these ageless, gothic arms. to rinse
his heart with a deluge of gin, call
lovers fools—but not you, not

you with your lacquered icons and aspic
lecterns. admit it. until footnotes
have heartbeats you'll need me
and you know it. and I'll

be here, the vengeful hem
of my dress an invitation
to let go the pound of smoke
holed up in your chest. to inhale

the abrupt musk of a woman
with edges like buck knives.
your restraint a trick of the liquor
coiled in your belly with the fear

and the want, a locked
vice icebox whose deadbolt
you lick clean every morning.

forgiveness
for Rev. L.

remember the boy you said
was only trying to get into my pants?
I almost married him. but there was a girl
at the bar with her back to me

and I couldn't breathe right. I had
then, so many hands. all aching toward
a pale landing strip of skin beneath
a dyed-black bob. is it possible

you felt the same way about God,
that God was a call more urgent
than your mother's? that everyone

you had been before fell out
of your hands, rose off your body
like water? the night that boy returned
to say, finally, that he wanted

only me, I was already gone. head full
of the call of a furious girl whose hands
would break me for any man for years,
whose neck haunts me in all

bars. you said *remember, God
loves you* with the conviction,
I recognize now, of a man

who's known sin. when you came
to the church where I was a girl
spinning in her choir robe, I heard
the congregation had expected

a wife also to arrive. small scandal.
I don't remember your hands. I do
remember the day I asked why
you hadn't gotten married again

and you said you were waiting
for me. and you laughed, and I did,
but I saw the skin under it. you never

said anything about sin, but when
this new love arrived on my tongue,
I stopped coming to visit. the boy
got divorced. you died

in the vestibule of the church
on a Wednesday, my mother running
from her classroom to shove her hands
again and again against your chest.

I didn't go the funeral. I was far away
and we hadn't spoken in years
though I'd thought of you often

whenever I was struck still
and wordless by some light
falling like God
across a woman's skin.

the fidelity of calendars

in the year of bad but necessary decisions
a boy I would later love yelled at me
for getting into the back of a pickup truck
driven by strangers with my little sister

in Wisconsin. it wasn't the smartest thing
I'd done to date, but certainly
the most entertaining. in the years
of drinking as the key to domestic tranquility

I tacked discount fabric to the walls
to cover the tangerine the previous tenant
had painted over the textured wallpaper. I went
to work every morning. at night the rats

would run the walls and if he were home
he might throw a shoe against the wall
to make them stop. often he wasn't
home. I'd let them run and run. the night

a black wool dress pressed against
the windows. we slept with the windows open
because we couldn't control the heat
in the years of constant overdraft, in the years

of mouths in stairwells, in the years of erupting
bookshelves and faces dissolving in acid
and powder my body grew a spongy,
undeliberate heart. my hands hung useless

at the ends of shrugging arms.
in the year of choosing love
over reason, I paid a stranger
to catalogue my stories while I cried

and blamed my parents. I lived above an alley
in an apartment painted yellow because it received
no natural light. it was my love's
dream home so we lived in it. when she left

I stayed for months, counting the seams
in the concrete ceiling. listening
to the trucks empty the dumpsters
every morning, every morning.

in the year of escape by any means necessary
I recovered my accent. started
believing in ghosts again. calling them
by my grandfather's name. in the year

of escape by any means necessary
again, I remembered my sister's face
as we climbed into the back of the pickup
driven by strangers. the wind on our necks

off the lake, how she hesitated at the tailgate
and looked at me, how she took the boy's hand
and stepped up and in, thinking, as I was, I'm sure of it,
we're together. what's the worst that could happen.

the fidelity of circumnavigation

I'm thinking I would like to be somebody else.
the last female matador. a door-to-door seller

of rhinestone-encrusted cupcakes. the boss asks
if I might consider taking one of the jobs

my co-workers are abandoning to snowshoe
across the arctic tundra or make ringtones

out of their baby's laughter. it's no laughing
matter. I came back to Chicago to become

a dolphin. no, I came to Chicago
to find a good chiropractor, so I could finally

turn my head all the way to the left. I came
for love. I came for the coffee. I came thinking

I left something here years ago, what was it, I can't
remember now, but it mattered, it was dazzling, be-

dazzled, I can see it out of the corner of my good
eye, it's out there on the lakefront, in the fountain

where the kids lay on their bellies and pretend
that they're mermaids, the water is filthy but everyone

pretends not to notice. that one kid is filling his mouth
up with water, spitting it like he's the fountain, the fish

at the top of the fountain leaning over, their mouths
green spouts for the water, full of pennies, full of children,

aren't there rules against that, against just getting
in the fountain in a diaper or barefoot, I remember

Denver, the middle of that road trip van-life summer,
have a picture of it, three of us hysterical in the fountain

in the middle of some festival, the children throwing water
everywhere around us, their appalled parents

in the background, thin dresses plastered
to our unwashed bodies, it was so hot that summer

and we'd stopped off-schedule and found
the festival, the fountain, it meant

we'd have to drive all night to make Chico
but it hardly mattered because that's

what we were looking for. that's what
I was leaving Chicago to find.

common denominators

in fractions, I always thought the dividing line
looked like a trampoline. my father
the accountant

disagreed. to him, it didn't matter
that the one seemed ready to jump
as far from the two

as possible. that the four could do
the limbo even with the three standing
on the broomstick. I

was always a little odd to my father
the accountant, the athlete. odd in that
it didn't matter

to me who won in soccer, so long as I didn't
lose my inhaler and the other team high-
fived me. I loved

the running and the kicking
but didn't care much about direction.
I scored once

on my own team. while playing
defense. no one yelled at me. I think
they thought

there was maybe something wrong
with me. when I was five, my father
ran the Boston Marathon.
it was hot and I wanted to leave. until

I was in my teens, the pressure from simply
diving into pool water

was enough to raise hot welts all over
my body. they sent me home
from kindergarten

thinking I had some disease. I was just glad
to see my mother. my father was at work,
or out running.

my mother used to run, but then she
had babies. eventually my father ruined
his knees. but he still

had math, still had his adding machine.
in his study, there were always shoes. a lamp
whose necked creaked

when it was moved and this is where he was assigned
to teach me math. Mom said numbers were not
my strong suit. but I did love

how the shelves seemed to straighten their shoulders
in that room. how the adding machine produced
its little stream of digits,

the paper a perfect coil just asking for a finger
but we're here for fractions. what is one half multiplied
by one fifth. what is two

fifths divided by seven tenths. what is a proper
fraction, improper, the numerator, subtraction
with like terms. with

unlike. mixed percentages, reciprocals. hello corkboard.
look how my dad has divided you into sections meant
for messages and sections

meant for work notes and sections for miscellaneous
reminders. I adore the word miscellaneous. I can even
spell it. *miscellaneous.*

numerator. my father is not happy. I am failing
the practice questions. the numbers go running.
his forehead is like

another mouth. both the mouths
are frowning. my father is an
accountant. he is

a runner. also I have heard him say he types faster
than his secretary. I would like to have a secretary.
I would ask her to do

my math for me. his watch shakes
its little glowing face. the wallpaper
picks at its

skirt, the penny jar rattles its quarters. he says
*let your mother help you. she can't do math
either.* the one

lays down on her black trampoline. *it's
a fraction bar*, I tell her. *get up.
don't be silly.*

the Empress is a drag queen

of course. what other mama's gonna love you
just the way you are? these things take time,
and care, you have to wait for the glue to dry
a bit before slapping on those lashes,

baby. just who are you aiming to be?
and why all this rush. there's always
another parade. another lover

when this one runs. you are your own
one, your own best love, you best
believe it before opening that door,
honey, before tossing your heart and all

the other parts in the ring. here's
the thing: you're a god. I'm a god.
we're all gods and worms, that's

the sweet stone truth. that's
what they'd have us forget. the wig,
the womb, it's all passage. choose
a great name. speak it like a prayer.

give yourself over to it like your love
of glitter and the great god whose body
men were always feeding you

in the cathedral, whose grape juice blood
you prayed would redeem you. make you
the boy your father wanted. the son
so full of the Holy Ghost there was no room

for want, for the belly-level tug of men
in their narrow pants, the call
of your mother's lipstick and pearls

from the bathroom cabinet, from the back
of her lingerie drawer where the jewelry sings
in a perfect contralto, a promise song
that you will be beautiful. you will be

stunning and accepted, a star. wheat
can't be blamed for the angle at which
it grows, any more than you can. lean

toward whatever water feeds you.
this isn't the easy road, but look
baby, look how it gleams.

when the one you thought, finally,
wouldn't, does,

where do you go? the hole in your hands
keeps getting bigger. first a pencil falls through.
then your teacup, then entire bodies

like light, like you're made of nothing stronger
than tissue, than sugar heated and spread
to look like glass. not the real thing. not you.
your atoms sit so far apart, your lovers

walk right through. one might say, over
the top of you. but no need for that, when you
can bend around their many departures, the most
porous door. she came back. they always

come back. why not. you are not a creature
of consequences. one way to survive a fall
is to believe very strongly that you
do not have bones. another

is to watch the hole in your body grow
until you are nothing but hole, and who
doesn't love a hole. you're the great circle
they can write their lives inside, a flat

unused womb they can crawl into. in this
way, you are useful. this way, you can sleep
in the house that raised you.

deliver us

there come such moments of redemption
and forgiveness that I can't imagine
saying another word about my father's infidelities

ever. the hypnotist doctoral student at the party
insists anything you say three times becomes true.
the limes on the bar peel back their skins

like a striptease. squeeze their way neatly
into my beer. I'm wearing rain boots
because I was on my way home

when the party erupted. now
there are magenta beverages
in every girl's hand. I notice

the toilet needs washing. this also
is not my problem. everything
the baby will be wearing must

be washed first with Ivory
Snow. there is no baby. my father
is in another city. lime, lime, lime.

•

what I know about solitude, I learned
by watching my father
wash dishes: cup, plate, knife, fork,
glass, spoon. she never left him

for good. I don't even like beer.
in the bathroom, someone

is painting the toilet magenta.
I am too old for the polite lies
that gap the minutes at parties.
I want a baby and everyone here

smells like latex. my parents bury
their sorrows under the hostas. bake it

into the skin of the chicken
then peel it off without eating. they wash
and wash and wash that old
bathtub, but it never looks clean.

•

you can get only so close without telling
the truth. saying something three times
makes it a toilet with a fluffy

magenta cover. which is better:
to be alone, or to own no footwear
but rain boots? once something

goes wrong, it almost always continues.
salt, tequila, lime. everybody keeps
getting younger except my father and I

who stand on opposite sides
of the El tracks waving and waving
and waving.

•

he wants to be close, but knows
what it costs. every month

I leave magenta streaks
on the ivory tiles. the cleaning lady

washes them up in a language I pretend
not to speak. limes shimmy

in the fridge. this is not
my house. but he lets me live here

because he loves me and it's his fault
I'm alive, my pink lungs

and rotten timing. what
I know about repetition, which is to say,

truth, I know from watching my father
wash dishes: cup, plate,

knife, fork, glass, spoon. she came
back. cup, plate, knife, fork, glass, spoon. it keeps

raining. cup, plate, knife, fork, glass, glass, glass,
spoon.

the fidelity of the ingrate

just when I think it can't get any worse,
I wake up still alive. still with this

river of grief clotted in my throat. ice wind
up the loose legs of my pants, alive. blown reflection

in the store windows, alive. January sun, slow train,
the alley home, alive. and I have no right

to be sad. I'm alive, no one
I love is dying, not any more

than usual. but there's an angry dog
about this morning. I leave the phone

unanswered for hours, the noise piling up
in my windpipe as people's lives

contort and resolve on the small screen. it's
a kind of relief, the pressure of making

no sound. watching fiction unwind. but I can't
stop looking at the shoes, the way they couple

and recouple, and it undoes me
each time. the walls are no comfort, stiff

in their salute of just going on, I want it all
to collapse. to come down on me, concrete

and steel and excuse, I want to stop.
there is wine, there are pills, there are clubs

full of bodies to grind this sorrow against
but it's all so alive with consequence and I want

not to die, exactly, but to pause all this feeling,
this relentless feeling, the exploding bird of my heart

taking up my whole insides with its enormous
flailing wings, its vacant, breathing, catastrophic mouth.

when it falls to you to love a liar

remember, you are happy. your life
a kite in a quiet park, the birds silent

in the hedges, the string
sending you over the trees,
everything below so small

you can barely make out the mouths.
close your eyes. the dogwood
does not smell like gasoline. remember

what you have learned about territory.
remember when you entered that grove

of microscopes, how terrifying
a simple skin cell looks at high
magnification. let's not do that

again. understand, it is your
feet that are on backward. your
organs disarrayed throughout

the torso. and yet your love
holds onto that string, sends

you flying. who else would do this
for you? you with your questions.
your plank of demands. the trees

below are so bright, they're bleeding.
their perfume is overwhelming.
all over the sky are kites

without strings, abandoned,
bird-torn and drifting. you're lucky.

look at your hand. look
at that ring. do it without blinking.

the fidelity of Oxford, Ohio

when my neighbor rings the doorbell
at 10 a.m. on a Sunday

to say my housemate's boyfriend
is passed out on her lawn again

I know it's time to graduate.
that I have sucked the marrow

out of this hambone town, grown
off the jutting hip of Kentucky.

I've done enough shots of Jager
to wake up in the bed of the assistant coach

of the wrestling team and despite
his devastatingly limited wit

dated him for two and a half weeks to prove
I was not easy. I have slept

in the library. I have slept
through chemistry. I have slept

on my best friend's floor which smelled
like drugstore perfume and stale pizza cheese

because someone swapped her heart
for scrap again and she swore

she wasn't lonely but she was gutted
like a melon and we were all out

of vodka. I go next door
to shove the snoring boy awake,

send him back to the fraternity
walking mostly sideways. it's Sunday

and I'm not done with 21. I've not yet
lived alone, not yet woken up in the bed

of a woman I love. the street is empty
as a 4 a.m. keg. the small yard

stretches out the length of my thumb.
I dump the ashtray over

the failing porch rail. I don't
even smoke. in Chicago, the boy

I intend to marry serves his seventeenth
latte of the day, paying close attention

to the foam, and not thinking
of me at all.

Nine of Rods watches too much
Law & Order

steam rises from my wet leg in the cold
October apartment. another month and ten
to fifteen degrees before the landlord
releases the heat. the third finger
of my left hand is a necrotic blue
where the pen bled out, *necrotic*

a word I learned from the TV
show about the girl tortured beyond
belief, showing just enough
for primetime, enough to wrestle
its way into my sleep because I didn't

turn away, hung on through the long shot
of the cops finding the chamber, the girl
alive in the drawer, her nails black, necrotic,
dying at the ends of her hands. the words
nuzzling their way into me, *sexual
sadist, serial killer, necrotic,* a world

whose door I slid just past as a kid, as
a girl, stalked by a man, the words *paranoid
schizophrenic* slipping around my ankles
like taffeta as I accelerated toward Ohio, away
from home and the neighbor with icebox eyes.

the stove is on and open, the heat of the almost
desperate and alone, dangerous maybe,
but not more than a day-long roast.
whatever's sacred about the human body
has to do with its ability to generate
heat, to keep on despite everything. the bath

starts to get cold, I'm no longer young, someone
on the street below is yelling, someone else
singing what could almost be a lullaby.
I turn off the stove, the night
goes on, we're all just a little on fire.

bargain

I am trying to patch together a life
that resembles less the handiwork

of a blind and distracted tailor.
I have not always made the best choices.

from here on in, I would like to make
different mistakes. my mother

was married before she could legally
drink. only the children in attendance

remember the champagne reception.
John says I can make love mean

whatever I want. tonight I want to kiss
impossible women everywhere. this

is not new, or different.
the first girl was a mermaid

in the play where I was the Indian
princess. I'm certain there was flesh

colored fabric between the seashells
and her tail, but all I remember

is skin. I was ten. all my friends were boy-
crazy so when they pressed the question,

I said *Tim Fitzgibbens* because he was blonde
and there. when the note came back checked

no, I was mortified, and forgiven. I can make
this mean whatever I want now. most

of the decks in Chicago are deathtraps
but nobody pays it much mind. to be

structurally sound is to subject
oneself to measurement. I'm bad

at the seams. I've given up on love.
or rather, love's going to have to find me

measuring fabric in the discount aisle. chugging
champagne at a stranger's wedding. giving

a baby an invented name. tell love
where I've gone. tell her not to come.

Three of Swords, again

just when I think this,
this is the last thing
between us, there's something

else. last night, in my drowned
and drunken mess of a heart,
I saw it: a knife. *a knife,*

I thought. *how obvious.*
have you been there all
along? yes, said the knife.

and I could only see
the tip of it, just the pointed
end sticking out. they say

girls always marry their fathers,
but here they're wrong. my
father stayed. you ran, your

schoolboy pants rolled high,
a pack of lies rectangling
your sleeve. all

your reasons for leaving
line up along the jutting ledge
of the blade and leap off. fact is,

you didn't fight for us. now for her,
you'll tie yourself into a ship's worth
of knots. maybe I wasn't busted

enough for you to be so careful
about me. maybe I invited this metal
into my body out of some twisted

martyr wish. but here's the thing,
maybe the last thing between us
at last. have your knife back. it's a little

bloody and rusted, but the name
on the handle is still legible
in good light. it's my father's,

of course. but you knew that.

the World's guide to beginning

I was born in the obscene genius
of the club. I was a chemical
hero. slick as a greasy encyclopedia,
I strutted like a bullfighter. I learned kink

is another word for survival. learned to love
the body more for what it can do
than for what it is. how did you get this far
without knowing lust is disaster's

good cousin, that lust flickers when the rest
has been burned down and blown
away? there will be a quiz.

here's another story: I was born.
I was adored. I am in charge. I need you
to tie me down, now. call it love,
this intimate vine. this gift

of the mother. gift of the neighbor, the uncle,
gift of the whip. the dildo. lying
was my first language. I am not ashamed.
touch is not reversible. do I make you

uncomfortable? good. then it's begun.
go ahead and cry. to break
is to be sanctified. to make in the body

a safehouse where all your monsters
get to be raucous, bring the audience
to their feet calling *what. what.*
dig at the shame places. your gutter

of a cunt. your crowbar of a cock.
say the words, say *fuck* and *wheelbarrow*
and *voluptuary* until it all sounds
like *amen, amen, amen, amen, amen,*

amen, amen, amen. why despise
your own wiring? it was desire
that made you; however corrupted

the originating bed, your beginning
was ferocious. what's the difference
between a lie and a myth? the storyteller's
intention. example: I am more bear

than fruit. more leather than lion.
legend says I opened my mouth
and the world rolled out. the brine
of saliva, brow bone splitting into branch,

into root. and from the cheeks, the sweetest
meat, the man, the woman, the lost
androgynous other. example: in our myth, Atlas

is a hermaphrodite. a dancer. a bearded lady
in a g-string in a cage above the dance floor.
fact: there are gods who love us, and they want
us to fuck. are you ready? have I earned

another story? to emerge, a world must learn
itself, then flood, then burn. unfurl your ugly
like a fist inside another's body.
step into a skin familiar

as your mother's bed. something in you
stands up. it is like light, or a crime.
it is alive. your turn.

Notes

Many of the poems in this book are framed using cards
from the traditional tarot deck. The tarot is a centuries-old
system of divination and self-discovery that uses visual
symbols, cues, and archetypes to tap into the connections
between an individual and the universe, her or his
subconscious, or wherever one believes free will and the
impetus for our life direction resides. The deck consists of
two primary parts, the Major Arcana and the Minor
Arcana. The Minor Arcana includes 56 cards divided into
four suits—Pentacles, Swords, Cups, and Rods—and
represents or indicates matters related to the energy,
activities, emotions, and people in our day-to-day lives.
The Major Arcana, made up of 22 cards such as the
Lovers, Temperance, the Chariot, the Empress, and so on,
illuminates and refers to issues of greater scale or
resonance, concepts and experiences outside of or in
some way deeply impacting our everyday lives.

Acknowledgments

Many thanks to the journals in which the poems below
previously appeared, some in different versions:

Beloit Poetry Journal: "when your grandmother mistakes
your girlfriend for a man"

Booth Magazine: "the Magician is a drag king,"
"Nine of Rods watches too much *Law & Order*"

Crab Orchard: "the fidelity of disagreement"

Drunken Boat: "the Chariot in love," "the World's guide
to beginning"

Indiana Review: "the fidelity of circumnavigation"

Muzzle Magazine: "the fidelity of calendars," "when your
ex-girlfriend's sister corners you in the kitchen"

Rattle: "fable telling how night invented herself out
of sound"

These poems and this book would not exist without the love
and support of so many people. First, my parents Sarah
and David, and my sisters Erin and Kristin, whose patience
and acceptance and belief in me has never failed. Thank
you. I love you. The people who took the time to edit the
book and its poems in so many forms and permutations:
Melody Jane Moore, John Paul Davis, Daphne Gottlieb,
Patrick Rosal, Roger Bonair-Agard, and Tristan Silverman.
The louderARTS Project and Vox Ferus communities, who
continue to move and push and inspire me. Rebecca Hart,
my tarot teacher and poem-series-jumpstarter and constant.
Mariah Neuroth, poem-tolerator, platonic life partner and
permanent tether. Emily and Geoff Kagan-Trenchard, Emily
Rose, Stacy Fox, Kim Tilford, Baz, Rachel McKibbens,
Jeanann Verlee, Caroline Harvey, and all my hearts all over
the country. My Morrigans, Andi Strickland, Heather
Gawronski-Salerno—we survived, and look what happened.

Gabrielle Bouliane, David Blair, Peter of the Earth, Kent
Foreman, Maria McCray: *I am living. I remember you.*

Marty McConnell earned her MFA at Sarah Lawrence College. Her poems have appeared in *Indiana Review, Crab Orchard,* and *Beloit Poetry Journal*, among others. A member of seven National Poetry Slam teams representing New York City and Chicago, she is a two-time recipient of the Community Arts Assistance Program grant from the City of Chicago's Office of Tourism and Culture. She is the founder of Vox Ferus, a Chicago-based nonprofit dedicated to empowering individuals and communities through the written and spoken word. She lives in Chicago. *wine for a shotgun* is her first book.